EXPERIENCING GOD

THE MUSIC

CREATED BY

Gary Rhodes AND *Claire Cloninger

WITH HENRY BLACKABY

A Worship Experience to Know and Do the Will of God

Orchestrations by:

Don Hart, Don Marsh, Steve Dunn, David Winkler, Kyle Hill, Jeff Cranfill

Products Available

Choral Book 0-6330-0693-9

Listening CD 0-6330-0710-2

Listening Cassette 0-6330-0709-9

Accompaniment CD 0-6330-0715-3 (Split-track)

Split-Track Accompaniment Cassette 0-6330-0713-7

Stereo-Track Accompaniment Cassette 0-6330-0734-X

Rehearsal Tracks 0-6330-0737-4

Orchestration 0-6330-0720-X

Invitation Video 0-6330-0730-7

Poster (Packs of 10) 0-6330-0731-5

Bulletins (Packs of 100) 0-6330-0732-3

Handbills (Packs of 100) 0-6330-0733-1

CD Promo Pak 0-6330-0722-6

Cassette Promo Pak 0-6330-0721-8

Instrumentation Includes: Flute 1-2, Oboe, Clarinet 1-2, Bassoon, Trumpet 1, Trumpet 2-3, French Horn 1-2, Trombone 1-2, Trombone 3/Tuba, Percussion 1-2, Timpani, Harp, Rhythm, Violin 1-2, Viola, Cello, String Bass

Substitute Parts: Alto Sax 1-2 (substitute for French Horn 1-2), Tenor Sax/Baritone Treble Clef (substitute for Trombone 1-2), Clarinet 3 (substitute for Viola), Bass Clarinet (substitute for Bassoon), Keyboard String Reduction

Claire Cloninger's involvement with this project is courtesy of Word Music.

GENEVOX

A Word From Henry Blackaby

When I first met with the design team and writers of this musical, my number one request of them was that they would speak truth. In this generation, music can be a huge conveyor of Truth, and when the Truth unchanged is communicated, God honors that and will transform lives in the process.

The prayer of all of us involved in the creation and production of this musical is that nothing in it would distract anyone from allowing God to bring him or her face to face with the cross, in all its intensity and passion. My desire is that this musical is always presented as an offering of worship to God. Our greatest desire is that God's people encounter Him in a life-transforming way. To that end, this entire endeavor is committed.

A Word From *Claire Cloninger

On the bottom shelf of my bedroom bookcase, resting out of sight, is a frayed and tattered workbook that I will never part with. It is a road map that traces the footsteps of my spiritual journey from where I was to where I am today. It is the workbook from my *Experiencing God* small group study. Because my relationship with God was so radically altered by this study group, I knew we would be working on something of major importance when I was asked to join Gary Rhodes in putting the vision of *Experiencing God* into a musical for choirs. More than anything, Gary and I wanted to be true to Henry Blackaby's God-given message, and I believe we have. This is a musical with heart, excitement, and vision.

Using music for adult and children's choir, solos, ensembles, narration, and monologue, the powerful message of *Experiencing God* is driven home. The music of *Experiencing God* delivers a call to the person in the pew to rise up out of the ordinariness of his Christian life and join the living God in the exciting work of reconciling the world to Himself. There is even a video-taped invitation given by Henry Blackaby.

Thanks be to God for men like Henry who have a heart to listen and the faith to obey. I am thankful for the tremendous gifts of Gary Rhodes, and for the guidance and support of the LifeWay creative team. I am also appreciative to my Word Music family who made it possible for me to be part of this project.

*Claire Cloninger's involvement with this project is courtesy of Word Music.

A Word From Gary Rhodes

Years ago, as a college student at Baylor University, I had the privilege of going on a mission trip to Faith Baptist Church in Saskatchewan where Henry Blackaby was Senior Pastor at the time. It was a life changing event for me. I was able to see and experience many of the things Dr. Blackaby would later share in *Experiencing God*. There was a sense of expectancy within the congregation, both corporately and individually, for what God was going to do in their midst. There was a seeking heart full of thankfulness with a constant recognition of God's love for them and what had been done on the cross. There was also a desire for relationship—to walk in purity before the Lord, always sensitive to His voice, wanting to hear Him and obey. Such an all-pervasive "Yes Lord!" filled the atmosphere that it was contagious. Thank You, Lord, for the mission trips You use to change our lives even more than the the lives of those people to whom we minister!

I can't express what an honor it has been to have the opportunity to be a part of taking Dr. Blackaby's life message and incorporating it into a musical. On an early June morning in 1999, several LifeWay Music Ministry employees, Claire Cloninger, and myself, were able, as a creative group, to sit and listen for a few hours to Dr. Blackaby share from his heart. He could have given an invitation right then and there and every one of us would have responded. God has given him the heart of a pastor toward the body of Christ—that truly our eyes would be open to see how deeply God loves us—to bring us each to a point where our only response to Him would be "Lord, You have captured my heart with Your love. I say 'yes,' Lord! I will follow You! Use me, send me!" It is our hope that God would use this musical to bring people into His presence—that each person would know that they are face to face with the living God and, in turn, would respond from the depths of their hearts. Thank You, Lord, for bringing my life full circle to a life that is bearing more fruit from seeds planted so long ago!

These last few months have been filled with trying circumstances in my life and that of my family. Over and over the Lord has brought to my mind things that I have meditated on from *Experiencing God*. Looking at each of these circumstances through the backdrop of the cross, knowing that He wants to walk with me through each step of the way, looking for what the Lord is doing in the midst of it all, keeping my heart before Him and in the Word, and weighing where I need to adjust and obey—all of these things have sustained me and my family through these difficult times. Thank You, Lord, for giving us what we need at just the right time!

So many people had a part in making this musical come to pass and reach its full potential in ministry!

• Henry Blackaby—Your passion to know the Lord is contagious; your humility and transparency are an inspiration.

• Claire Cloninger—You made this a musical soaked with the heart of God.

• LifeWay employees (too many to list)—You have a great team dedicated to the creation of life–changing products for His glory.

• My family—Your patience, love and support encompass all that this musical is about.

• Prayer partners (too many to list)—You laid the foundation; you fought the battle. May the Spirit of God touch and forever change life after life.

• Technical staff—This musical would not have materialized without the dedication of many people involved in its recording and production (orchestrators, engineers, players, studio singers, Waco choir members, transcribers, editors, artists).

My wife is convinced that most people have no idea what goes into a musical like this. We all desire that this musical would bring honor and glory to You, Lord—You have been the inspiration for us all. We love You!

CONTENTS

Name of Names

Words by
CLAIRE CLONINGER

Music by
GARY RHODES
Arranged by Gary Rhodes

With great meaning ♩ = 85

*WHEN I SURVEY THE WONDROUS CROSS (O Waly Waly - Early American folk tune)

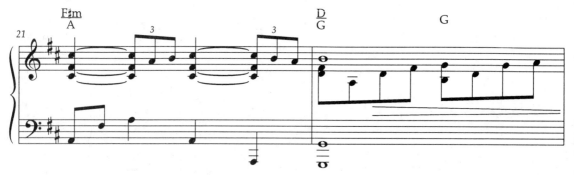

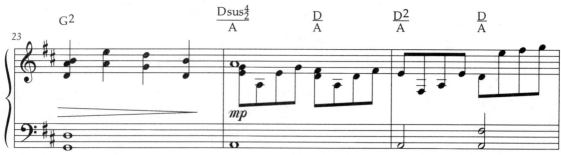

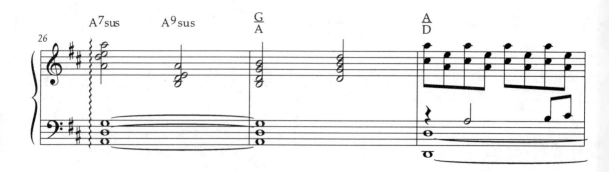

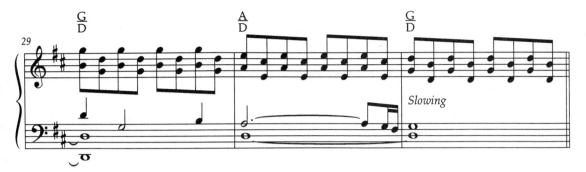

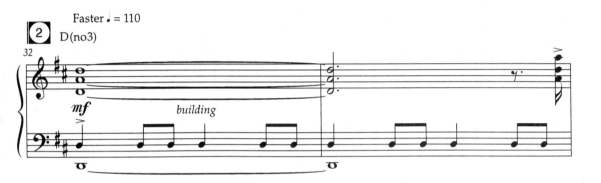

*VOICE OF GOD:** Moses, take off your shoes, for the ground on which you stand is holy ground.

"Voice of God" appears at end of accompaniment tracks.

each time they gave Him an - oth - er name!

The more He chose to show them, the more they came to know Him,

each time they gave Him an - oth - er name! De -

*VOICE OF GOD: Noah, build yourself an ark for your family, and bring aboard two of **every** living creature for I am going to flood the earth.

When No - ah heard the voice of __ God, __
To A - bra - ham, God said, "A - rise, __

he built an ark to sur - vive the __ flood. __
and take your son as a sac - ri - fice." __

He car - ried out the Lord's com - mand; __
So A - bra - ham did what God __ said __

and soon the ark was up-on dry land.

and God pro-vid-ed a ram in-stead!

(Worship Leader begins) "Again and again..."

WHEN I SURVEY THE WONDROUS CROSS
(Isaac Watts/Appalachian Folk melody)

WORSHIP LEADER: Again and again, God revealed Himself to human beings, and each time they gave Him a name based on that revelation. David called Him "our Strength," Jeremiah called Him "our Comforter," and Job called Him "my Friend." All of these names were true of God, and all of them pointed to Jesus. Jesus is the one Isaiah spoke of when he prophesied "A virgin will give birth to a son and call his name Immanuel."

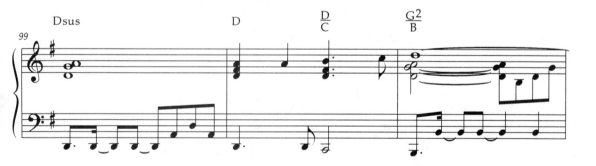

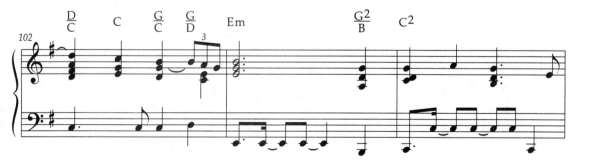

Underscore 1 (Speechless)

Arranged by Gary Rhodes

WORSHIP LEADER: *(music starts)* God has been at work throughout history pursuing a relationship with human beings. In burning bushes, on blazing mountaintops, in silent rooms and quiet moments, God has been drawing people to Himself. Can you imagine Moses or Mary, Abraham or Noah as they actually came into contact with the Living God? He revealed Himself in a unique way to each of them, and in turn they each responded differently. Some trembled, some bowed down, some stood before Him in silent awe. How would you have responded? How we respond to God reveals what we believe about Him.

Speechless
(Male trio or soloist with Choir)

Words and Music by
STEVEN CURTIS CHAPMAN and GEOFF MOORE
Arranged by Gary Rhodes

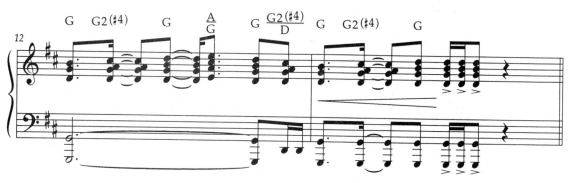

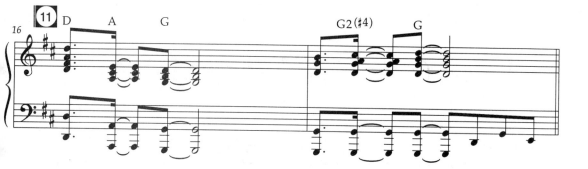

Words fall— like drops of rain,—

my lips are— like clouds.

I say— so— man-y things

try - in'— to fig - ure— You out!

But as mer - cy o - pens— my eyes, and

my words— are stol - en— a - way_____ with this

breath - tak - ing view of—Your grace. And I am

speech - less,— I'm a - ston - ished and— a - mazed!— I am

si - lenced— by Your won - drous— grace!— You have

28

God of— this whole u - ni - verse!———

It's a

sto - ry— that's too great— for— words!—

And I am

saved_____ me,_____ You have raised_____ me__ from__ the__

saved_____ me,_____ raised_____ me__

Dsus$^4_2$ D $\frac{Em}{B}$ Bm^7

grave!_____ And I am

from the__ grave!_____

G^2 G $\frac{G2(\#4)}{A}$ G   A   G $\frac{G2(\#4)}{A}$

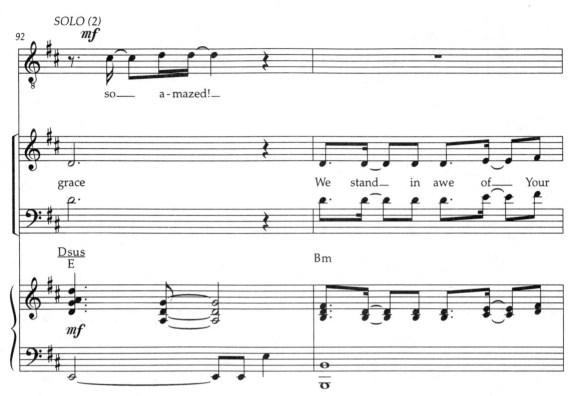

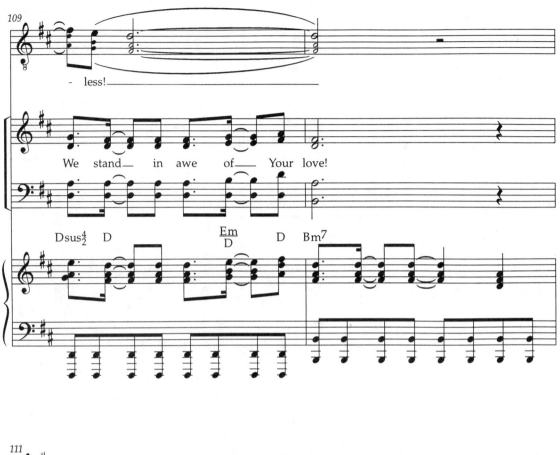

109

- less!

We stand in awe of Your love!

Dsus$\frac{4}{2}$ D Em/D D Bm7

111

We are speech - less!

D/G Em/G G G2(♯4) G A/G G G2(♯4)

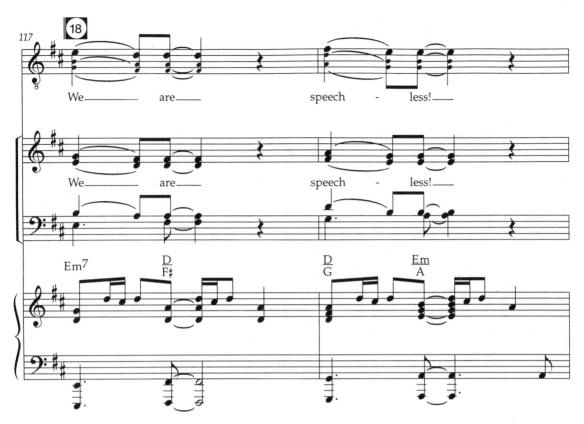

We _____ are _____ speech - less! _____

We _____ are _____ speech - less! _____

Em7   D/F#   D/G   Em/A

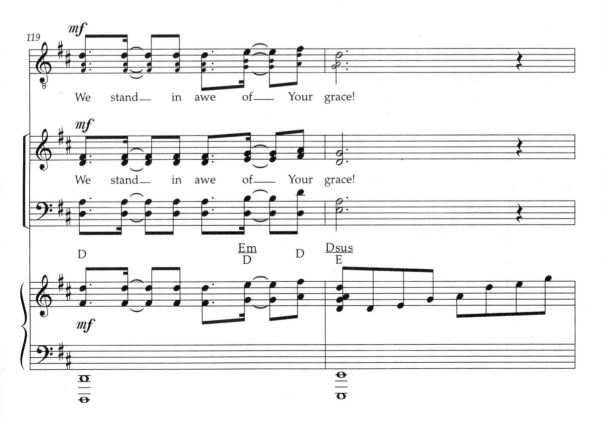

We stand __ in awe of __ Your grace!

We stand __ in awe of __ Your grace!

D   Em/D   D   Dsus/E

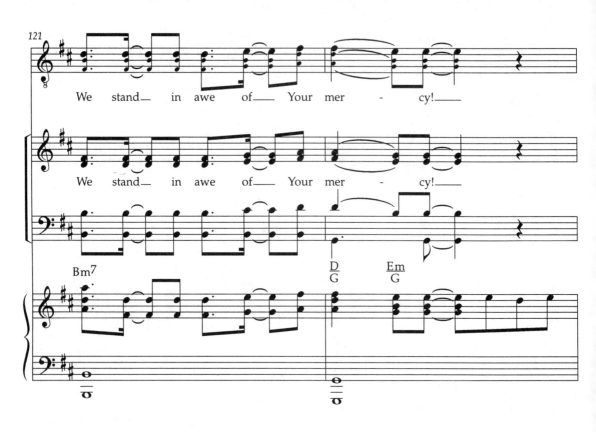

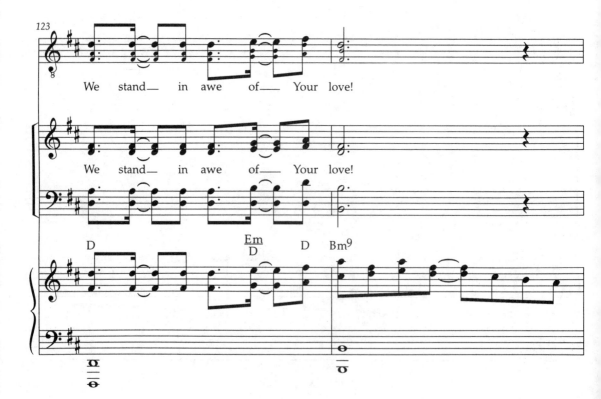

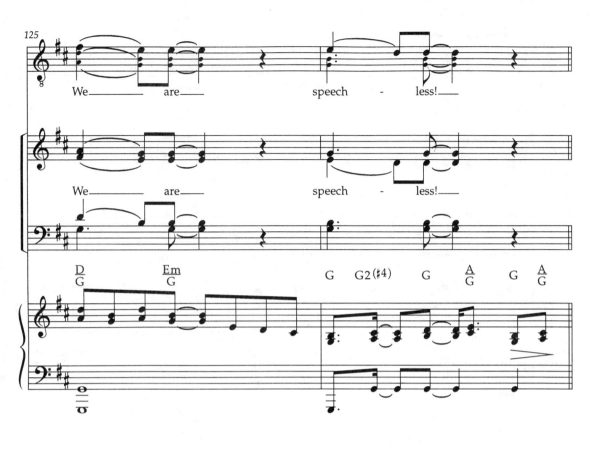

We stand__ in awe of__ Your pow - er!__

We stand__ in awe of__ Your pow - er!__

slowing

We__ are__ speech - less!__

slowing

We__ are__ speech - less!__

slowing

p

Stay up

Eyes of Your Heart

Words by
CLAIRE CLONINGER

Music by
GARY RHODES
Arranged by Gary Rhodes

WORSHIP LEADER: ***(without music)*** Here in this place, God is doing what only ***(music begins)*** He can do. He's pursuing a relationship with you. If you've never known Him before, you can begin to know Him now. If you've known Him for many years but have hungered for something deeper, that's exactly what He's holding out to you. It may surprise you to know that people have been praying for you—that during this presentation your life would be transformed. If you're willing for that to happen, it can. If you're willing to forget about the past—to let go of the future and just meet God in this moment, you will find Him here. His Holy Spirit is waiting to be our guide into the awesome majesty of His presence. Are your eyes open to see Him? Ah, is your heart open to receive? As the choir sings a prayer over us now, let's be truly open to see God and receive all that He has for us.

Tenderly ♩ = 85
*OPEN OUR EYES, LORD (Robert Cull)
"He's pursuing a relationship with you..."
D
Dsus/E
D/F♯
G2(♯4)
G
Em/A
p
5
A
Bm7
A7/C♯
Dsus4/2
D
A/C♯
Bm
9
D/A
Dsus4/2/A
D/A
Gmaj9
Em
A
13
Bm7
A7/C♯
Dsus4/2
D

52

If multiple instruments are being used, the introduction for "Open the Eyes of My Heart" may start under this sustained chord.

Open the Eyes of My Heart

with

Be Thou My Vision

(Choir with Congregation and optional Praise Team)

Words and Music by
PAUL BALOCHE
Arranged by Gary Rhodes

With pulse and energy! ♩ = 107-110

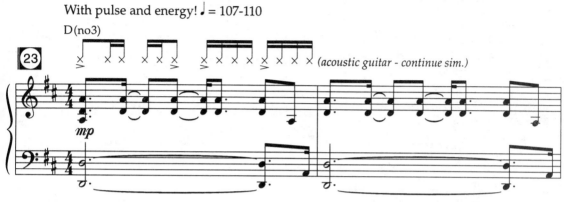

62

see You!___ I want to see You!___

Be Thou my___ Vi - sion, O Lord of my heart;

*BE THOU MY VISION (Traditional Irish words and melody)

My Abba's Child

with

Abba Father

(Children's Choir, Choir, Male Solo, and Congregation)

Words by
CLAIRE CLONINGER

Music by
GARY RHODES
Arranged by Gary Rhodes

*WORSHIP LEADER: *(prays as music begins)* God, push aside every competing distraction. Let us look directly into the loving face of our Savior, and once our eyes are open we can see that we have been blessed with every spiritual blessing. Thank you for choosing us before the creation of the world to be adopted as Your sons and daughters through Jesus. This is Your pleasure and this is Your will—to know us and love us intimately, as a father loves his child. *(segues into Child's speech)*

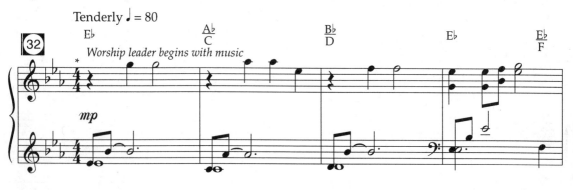

*Children's Choir softly moves into place.

CHILD: Because we are God's children, He has sent the Spirit of His Son, Jesus, into our hearts, so that now we have the right to talk about God as our Father, our Abba... our Dad. (Galatians 4:6)

Standup

25

and You hear me. I call, You're by my side.

D   D/F#   Gm   Fm7   B♭7sus

28

I fall, You lift me. I call,

CHOIR
p

Ooo

E♭   A♭2/C   A♭/C   B♭/D   B♭7/D

*WORSHIP LEADER: Sometimes a picture is worth a thousand words. At the 1992 Olympics in Barcelona, spectators saw a living picture of God's love for His children. That year, Derek Redmond of Great Britain was reaching for his lifelong dream of winning a gold medal in the four-hundred-meter run. As the gun sounded for the semi-finals, Derek knew without a doubt he was running the race of his life. Then, tragically, a torn right hamstring sent him sprawling facedown on the hard surface of the track. By a sheer act of will, he struggled to his feet and began crazily hopping toward the finish line. Suddenly a large man in a T-shirt bounded out of the stands, flinging security guards aside. Making his way toward the wounded runner, Jim Redmond threw his arms around his son.

"Son, you don't have to do this," he said.

"Yes, Dad, I do," Derek answered.

"All right then, let's finish this thing together," said the older man. And that's exactly what they did. Staying in Derek's lane the whole way, the son's head frequently buried in his father's shoulder, they made it to the end of the race as the crowd rose to its feet, weeping and cheering!

Derek Redmond did not win the gold medal that day. But he walked away from the race with the memory of a father who loved him too much to stay in the stands watching him suffer—a father who came down out of the stands and entered his race. This is the kind of heavenly Father we have, One who loves us too much to look down from heaven watching us fall and fail, but who is willing to come into our race, running it beside us and within us every step of the way until we are safely home.

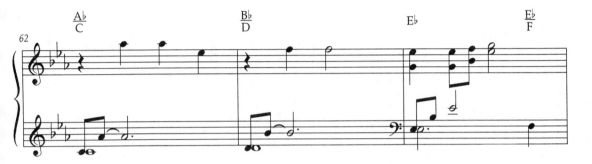

"All right then, let's finish this thing together..."

76

"But he walked away from the race..."
*SPEECHLESS (Steven Curtis Chapman/Geoff Moore)

WHEN I FALL (Claire Cloninger/Gary Rhodes)

When I fall, You re-store me, and when I fail You lead me in Your way! When the

Ooo

Children's Choir

82

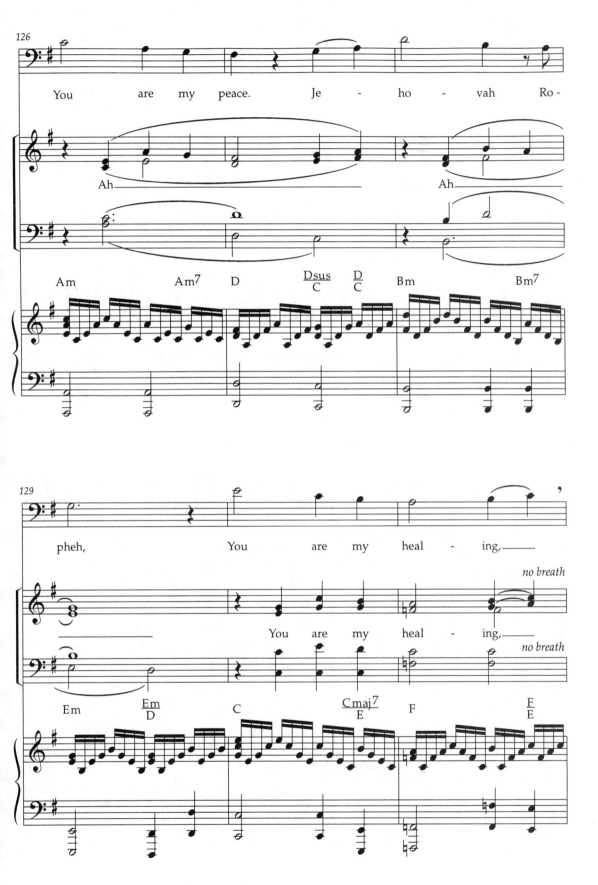

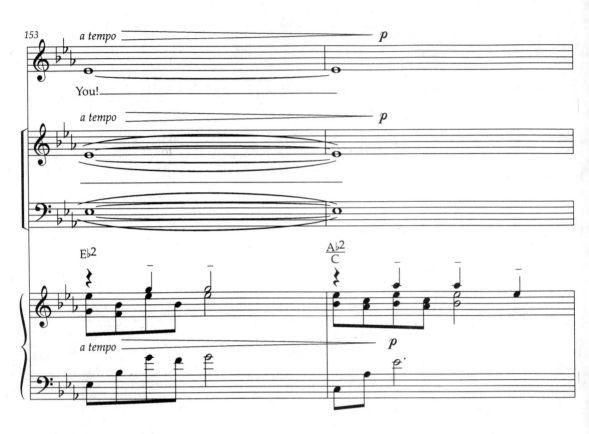

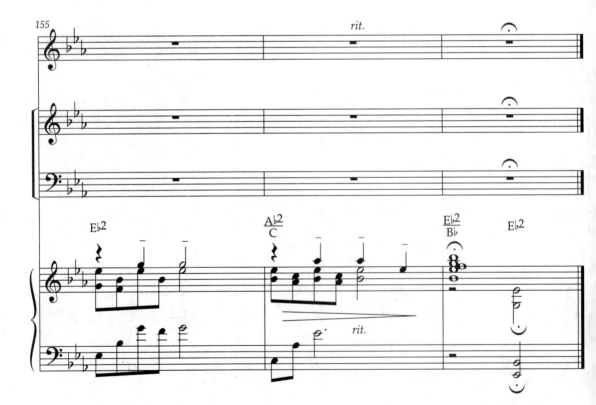

What Is Jesus Doing?

with

Sometimes by Step

Trio (youth) with Choir and Congregation

Words by
CLAIRE CLONINGER

Music by
GARY RHODES
Arranged by Gary Rhodes

WORSHIP LEADER: *(music begins)* How awesome to know that the God of the universe wants to have a Father/child relationship with us! He's inviting us to join Him in the work of reconciling the world to Himself. When God came to Moses or Abraham or the disciples, He didn't ask, "What would you like to do for Me?" He already had a plan. And they each had to make some major adjustments before He could work that plan out in their lives. God still operates that way. He's not asking us, "What would you like to do for Me?" He's already got a plan. And if we let Him, He is more than able to carry out His plans in us and through us.

*Two girls and one guy or three girls.

wants to do—through—you.—
got one of— His— own.—
It's not some pow - er of— your own,
It's not your gifts— you give— to Him;—

Ooo—

hoo—

Eb2/G Eb/G Ab Ab2 Eb/G

DUET (Female/Male)

it's His pow - er flow - ing through.—
for they come— from Him— a - lone.—
It's not what He—
If you put down—

Ooo—

Bbsus Bb Ab/Bb Bb Ab/Bb Bb Eb/Bb Eb

(Would work with two girls also.)

†SOMETIMES BY STEP (David Strasser/Rich Mullins)

CHOIR with Congregation *f*

O God, You are my___

Youth group enters passing out WIJD? (What Is Jesus Doing) bracelets as they sing.

step by step You'll lead me and I will fol-low You all of my

days! Yes, step by step You'll lead me and I will

fol-low You all of my days!

Underscore 2/(On My Knees)

Female Solo with Choir

Arranged by Gary Rhodes

WORSHIP LEADER: *(prays **without** music)* Lord God, You know the desire of our hearts is to follow You where You lead us. The longing in each of us is to know You, to hear Your voice, to encounter You in a meaningful way. Thank You, Lord, *(music begins)* that You are here tonight. Amen.

(To congregation) You know, the deep longing we feel to encounter God is actually the beginning of the encounter itself, for only God can place that longing in our hearts. We don't have to strain our ears to hear Him. He's always speaking to us.

For instance, have you ever been reading the Bible when suddenly you are gripped with a fresh new understanding? That was God speaking! When this happens, write it down, meditate on it, immerse yourself in it. Ask God to show you what adjustments you need to make to bring your life in line with it. Then make those adjustments, and watch to see how God uses it.

God also speaks to us through His body, the church. The members of Christ's body guide His church in the same way that the members of the human body guide the body. For example, suppose you were walking down a train track when suddenly your ears informed you that a train whistle was blowing somewhere very near. Then your feet warned you of the rumbling motion of an approaching train. Wouldn't you get off those tracks as soon as possible? Well, we in the church can learn to trust each other in exactly this same way.

The most important way we hear from God is when we enter His presence to pray. There is no substitute for prayer. There's no way to be in God's presence and remain unchanged. Prayer is a two-way communication with God in which listening is more important than talking. As we pray, the Holy Spirit leads us into all truth, but truth is not just a concept. Truth is a person. To pray is to know Jesus Christ, who is Truth.

With much emotion ♩=92

51 *THY WORD (Michael W. Smith/Amy Grant)

New tempo ♩ = 64

**WE ARE THE BODY OF CHRIST (Scott Wesley Brown/David Hampton)

52 A(no3) "...suppose you were walking..."

***Train sounds appears at the end of accompaniment tracks.

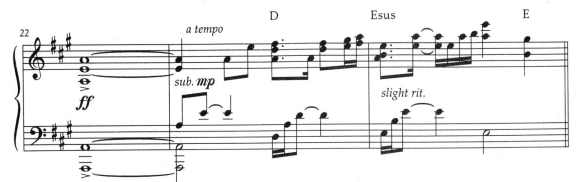

LORD, LISTEN TO YOUR CHILDREN PRAYING (Ken Medema) "...there is no substitute..."

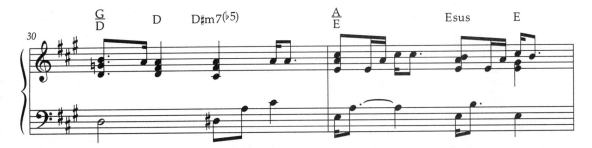

"...who is Truth."

On My Knees

Words and Music by
NICOLE COLEMAN-MULLINS, DAVID MULLINS,
and MICHAEL HUNTER OCHS
Arranged by Gary Rhodes

let-ting go___ and soar-ing on___ the wind. 'Cause I've learned in

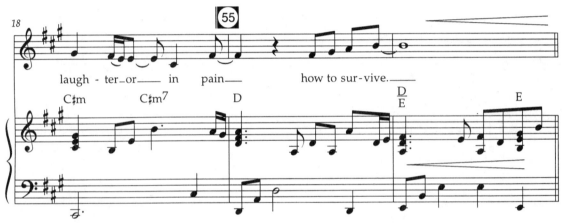

laugh-ter_or___ in pain___ how to sur-vive.___

I get on my knees,___ I get on my

LADIES unison

I get on my knees,___

110

116

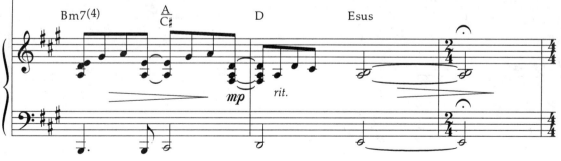

When I Survey the Wondrous Cross

Words by
ISAAC WATTS

Music : O WALY WALY
(Early American folk tune)
Arranged by Gary Rhodes

WORSHIP LEADER: *(music begins)* God can also speak to us through our circumstances, the good things and the bad. But we need to be careful not to judge Him from the middle of the bad things. This was a lesson Henry Blackaby experienced first hand when his child was diagnosed with cancer at age sixteen. "We suffered as we watched the sickness that goes along with chemotherapy and radiation," Blackaby said. "Some people face such an experience by blaming God and questioning—why doesn't He love me any more? The cancer treatments could have been very devastating for us. But did God still love us? Yes, He did. Had His love changed? No, it had not. When you face circumstances like this, you can question and ask God to show you what is going on. We did that. We had to ask Him what we should do. We asked all those questions, but I never said, 'Lord, I guess you don't love me.' At times I went before the heavenly Father, and I saw behind my child the cross of Jesus Christ, and I said, 'Father, don't ever let me look at my circumstances and question Your love. Your love for me was settled on the cross. That has never changed and it never will.'"

With great meaning ♩ = 80

WHEN I SURVEY THE WONDROUS CROSS (Isaac Watts/Lowell Mason)
WORSHIP LEADER: "God can also speak..."

"The cancer treatments..."

*MY ABBA'S CHILD (Claire Cloninger/Gary Rhodes)

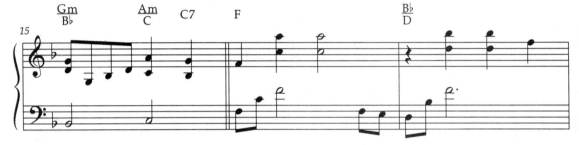

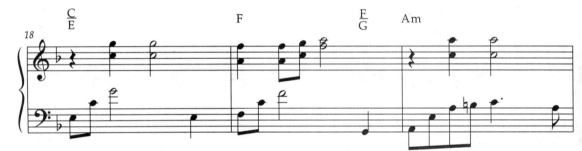

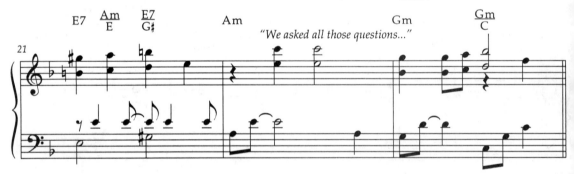

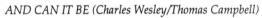
AND CAN IT BE (Charles Wesley/Thomas Campbell)

"...and it never will."

LADIES unison
with depth of heart

When I sur - vey   the won - drous

cross   On which the Prince

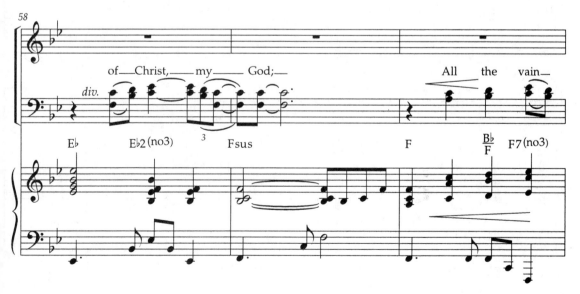

*Hammer hits appear at the end of the accompaniment tracks.

love— flow— min - gled— down;—

Did e'er such— love— and— sor - row

Did e'er such love,— such love and— sor - row

meet,

meet,— Or thorns com - pose—

*SPEECHLESS (Steven Curtis Chapman/Geoff Moore)

†If rhythm is too difficult, play all eighths in left hand.

Henry Blackaby's personal invitation to respond to the message of "Experiencing God" has been captured on a video recording and is available specifically for use with this musical. Please refer to the "Invitation" section of the Production Notes in the back of this book for suggestions on maximizing the impact of this moment.

A piano transcription of the underscore used on the video appears on page 168.

Use Me, Send Me

with

Just As I Am

Song of Invitation
Choir and Congregation

Words by
CLAIRE CLONINGER

Music by
GARY RHODES
Arranged by Gary Rhodes

*Choir should feel free to respond to the invitation during this time.

132

*Verse 2 lyrics by Claire Cloninger.
© Copyright 2000 Word Music (a div. of WORD MUSIC)/Juniper Landing Music (adm. by WORD MUSIC)/ASCAP.

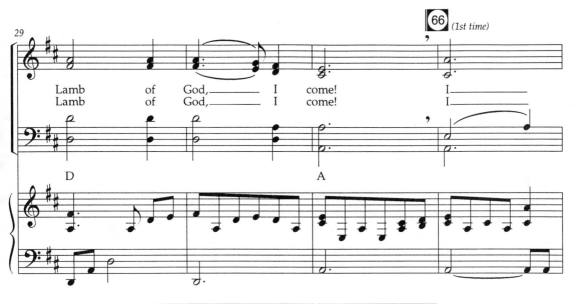

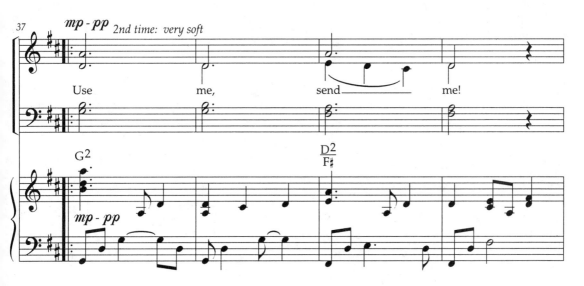

Segue to "Have Thine Own Way"

Have Thine Own Way

with

Have Your Way in Me and The Potter's Hand

Solo with Choir and Congregation

Arranged by Gary Rhodes

HAVE YOUR WAY IN ME (Claire Cloninger/Gary Rhodes)

Je - sus have Your way in me.

HAVE THINE OWN WAY, LORD (Adelaide A. Pollard/George C. Stebbins)

27 *mp* Female SOLO (1st time)

1. Have Thine own way, Lord! Have Thine own

1st time: CHOIR sing "Ooo"
2nd time: CHOIR sing lyrics

Ooo
2. Have Thine own way, Lord! Have Thine own

Slightly faster (♩ = 76)

Female SOLO

Beau-ti-ful Lord,— won-der-ful Sav - ior, I know for sure— all of my days— are held in Your hand;—

crafted in-to___ Your per - fect plan.___

1st time: CHOIR joins Soloist
2nd time: add Congregation

You gen-tly call___ me in - to Your pres - ence, guid-ing me by___

mold me,_____ use me,_____ fill me;_____ I

give my life_____ to_____ the Pot - ter's hand._____

Call me,_____ guide me,_____ lead me,_____ walk be -

146

side me;___ I give my life___ to___ the Pot - ter's hand..

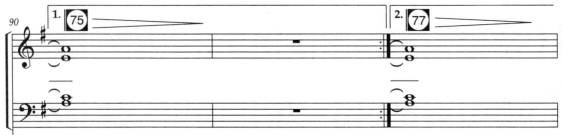

Bm/E   Em7   F   C/E   Am/E   Em7

1. 75   2. 77

1. Am   G2/B   Dsus   D   2. Am   G2/B

Dsus   D   G   D/F#

Slightly slower
mp

Take me,___ mold me,___

mp

give my life to the Pot - ter's hand.

F C/E Em7 Am G2/B

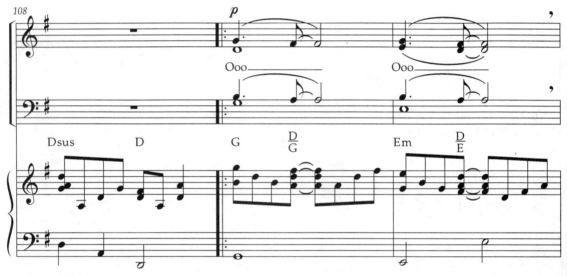

Ooo Ooo

Dsus D G D/G Em D/E

2nd time: poco a poco rit.

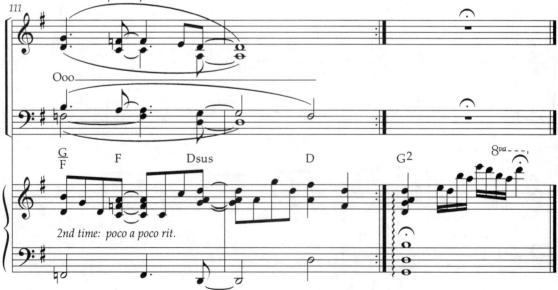

Ooo

G/F F Dsus D G2

2nd time: poco a poco rit.

Finale

with
I Will Never Be the Same Again, Name of Names, Speechless, and When I Survey the Wondrous Cross

Arranged by Gary Rhodes

WORSHIP LEADER: *(speaks to audience)* Here in God's presence (tonight) He's opened our eyes to who He is and how much He loves us. Let's join hands right where we are now and open ourselves to Him. *(music begins)*

(prays) Oh Lord, You have captured our hearts with Your love! You have opened our eyes to the reality of who You are, and we are in awe of Your mercy, that You would send Your own Son to die for us, that You would welcome us into Your presence as Your sons and daughters, that You hear us when we pray and lift us when we fall, and call us into a relationship with You. Oh God, we see so clearly that there is no life apart from You, and we choose this day to love You and follow You. There will be no turning back. Our lives are in Your hands.

150

*I WILL NEVER BE THE SAME AGAIN (Geoff Bullock)
1st time: CHOIR unison
2nd time: parts

I will nev-er be the same a-gain.

I can nev-er re-turn, I've closed the door.

flow like might-y wa - ters, a-gain and a - gain;___

Sweep a-way___ the dark - ness, burn a-way___ the chaff,___ and

let a flame burn___ to glo-ri-fy___ Your___ name!

I will nev-er be _____ the same _____ a - gain, _____

I can nev-er re-turn, _____ I've closed the _____ door. _____

I will walk the path, _____ I'll run the _____ race, _____ and I

*NAME OF NAMES (Claire Cloninger/Gary Rhodes)

158

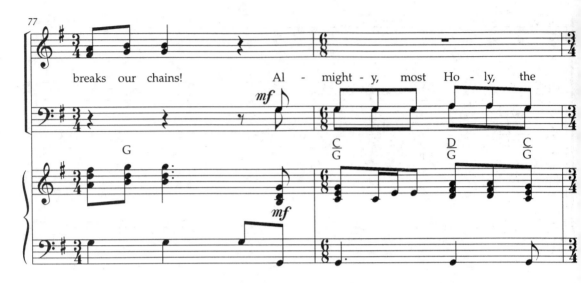

104

shown— us,—   leaves— us,—

shown——— us— a love that leaves——— us—

Dm   C/D   C/E   Dm/F   C/G   Csus/G

106   85   *end SOLO*

— whoa,— speech - less!—

Broadening

speech - less!—
unis.

Csus⁴₂   C   Csus⁴₂

Broadening and cresc.

*WHEN I SURVEY THE WONDROUS CROSS (Isaac Watts/O Waly Waly - Early American folk tune)

Invitation: Underscore

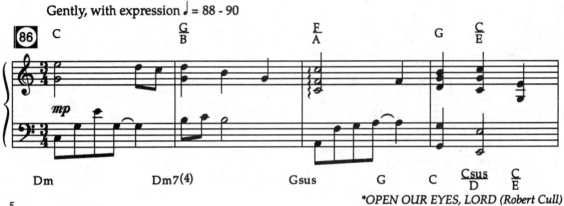

OPEN OUR EYES, LORD (Robert Cull)

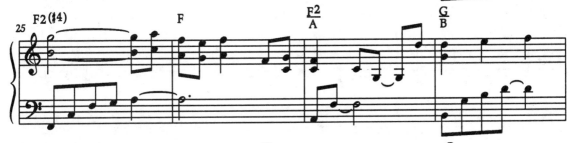

*WHEN I SURVEY THE WONDROUS CROSS (O Waly Waly)

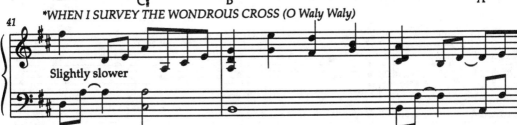

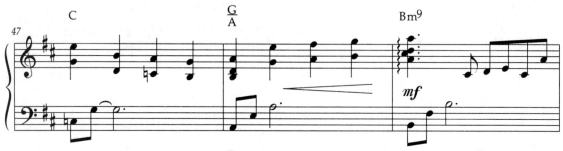

OH, MY JESUS (Gustav Holst)

Slower ♩ = 72

WHEN I SURVEY THE WONDROUS CROSS *(Isaac Watts/Lowell Mason)*

172

BE THOU MY VISION (Traditional Irish words and melody)

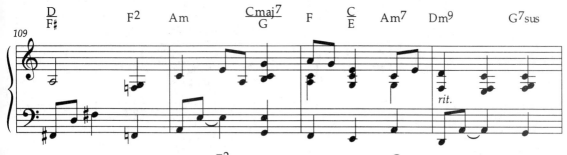

THE POTTER'S HAND (Darlene Zschech)

EXPERIENCING GOD
Production Notes
By Claire Cloninger and Gary Rhodes

Production Approach

Experiencing God differs from other choir musicals in a number of ways.

1. It's message is primarily to the church, although it does hold out a strong evangelical call to nonbelievers, as well.

2. It uses performance songs, personal worship with audience participation, as well as sharing of the basic principles of the *Experiencing God* program to draw the listener into a deep personal relationship with God.

Experiencing God can be performed as part of a morning or evening worship service or presented as a special program. Should you choose to use it in the normal worship service, we suggest that you clear the decks of as much additional agenda as possible, leaving adequate time to present the musical in the fullness of its form and in the depth of its call.

The Narrator/Worship Leader

The Narrator should have the heart of a Worship Leader as he will be operating in that capacity during much of the musical. It is also important that this person have the ability to time the spoken word with the musical underscore. The underscore is written in such a way as to heighten the meaning of the spoken message. Adequate rehearsal time should take care of this concern. This role is by far the largest, and therefore one of the most important in the production. Memorization of lines will greatly enhance the effectiveness of the Narrator/Worship Leader's part. He or she should also be on a wireless microphone which will supply freedom of movement.

Worship Team, Ensemble, Soloists, and Children's Choir

The worship team, ensemble, and soloists will, in all probability, be part of the choir as a whole. Depending on the number of microphones available, and the staging of the individual songs, the worship team, ensembles, and soloists could use standing microphones or wireless ones. The children's choir will be brought in from off stage and should be amplified as a group once onstage.

Visual Media

Experiencing God can be richly augmented by the use of visual media. You should begin right away to collect your own assortment of visual images. Slides, videos, and projected lyrics are among a number of visual aids you may employ. Also, the use of banners, a colorful addition to any presentation, are very appropriate during this musical.

Sound Effects (included on the accompaniment tracks)

There are several sound effects included on the CD and cassette accompaniment track that can be used when presenting *Experiencing God* with a live orchestra. These include:

1. Voice of God: Used as notated in "Name of Names" at measures 36 and 76.

2. Train Sounds: Used as notated in "On My Knees," measure 20.

3. Hammer Hits: The most flexible way to include this sound is to either produce it live with a hammer striking an anvil, doing the crucifixion scene live with the cross, or sampling the hammer hits on the track and playing it on beat one of each measure of "When I Survey" from measures 72-84. The difficulty with using the track only with a live orchestra will be synching up the track sound with the live orchestra and continuing in synch for 12 measures. One other way to accomplish this would be to cue up the hammer strikes and play it on beat one of measure 72, reset, play it again on beat one of 73, and so on.

Drama

Drama, especially pantomime, could be used successfully in several places within the musical. Specific ideas will be given in the song-by-song suggestions below.

Set

Experiencing God requires no specific set. The stage or sanctuary could be made visually appealing by using artistically draped swags of fabric. A large assortment of well-placed greenery also makes a pleasing backdrop. Banners are very impressive. You may consider creating one large banner displaying the cover logo and lettering of the *Experiencing God* songbooks. This would set the stage beautifully. Other suggestions for set design will be supplied along with the song-by-song production ideas below.

Lighting

Experiencing God could conceivably be presented with general sanctuary lighting only, but the ability to darken or spotlight areas of the stage, and the ability to use follow spots on individual performers, will add dramatic focus to the production. You may choose to bring up house lights during the audience participation sequences so that audience members will feel a part of what is taking place on stage. Should you plan to use slides and/or overhead projections of lyrics, make sure you are able to darken your room sufficiently to make them visible. Other occasional lighting suggestions are included with production ideas below.

Additional Suggestions for Using the Musical in Your Church

1. The music minister may choose the date of his/her presentation of the musical to tie in with the *Experiencing God* program— either before the program is offered, as a way of stirring up interest; or after the program has been completed, as a culminating activity. Either way, the musical can heighten the message and effectiveness of the program itself.

2. The music minister may choose to teach some or all of the worship choruses used in the musical to the congregation ahead of time so that church members will be familiar with the group-participation songs when the musical is presented.

3. During the weeks preceding the musical presentation, the pastor may wish to have one or more church members who have gone through the *Experiencing God* program give brief personal testimonies in the Sunday morning or evening services of how God worked in their lives through the program. These testimonies can serve as reminders of the upcoming musical presentation, and can also create interest in future offerings of the program itself.

4. The music minister may wish to consider presenting *Experiencing God* in collaboration with one or more other churches in the area. This kind of joint effort promotes unity in the body and can be a tremendous outreach to the community.

SONG–BY–SONG PRODUCTION IDEAS

"Name of Names"—The opening sequence of any musical is of utmost importance dramatically. It gives the audience it's first impression of the musical and should help them catch the vision of what will follow. Three different suggestions for the opener follow.

1. If an Irish Flute soloist is available, the choir could be in place, lights down, with a spot on the soloist. Then as the whole orchestra comes in, lights come up full.

2. The opener could be used as a procession piece for the choir to enter. This song is a very visual description of God revealing Himself to people throughout history. We would encourage you to put together video clips of everything from *Prince of Egypt* to *Exodus* in order to illustrate the lyrical content of the song. Or it could open with a live pantomime of Moses standing before the burning bush. Then as the verse begins, the spot could fade on him and the video could begin. Slides of still photos would also work well. Another visual possibility might be brought in during the part of the song which addresses the birth of Jesus. This scene could be staged live with your drama team.

3. A third option is that the choir processes in during the first verse and chorus of the song. Then banners proclaiming the names of God could be used effectively during the final choruses of "Name of Names" since the lyric of the chorus voices some of the different names of God. *Note: We are also suggesting the use of banners during the "Name of Names" reprise in the finale. This use of banners at the beginning and the end supplies a "book-end" dramatic effect that works well. You*

may, however, wish to save the drama of your banners for the finale, alone.

"Speechless"—As the opening song ends, lights go down on the choir during the "tag" (the last few measures after big cut-off note). The spot then comes up on the Narrator/Worship Leader. After the Narrator has spoken, lights go down on him and the spot comes up on the "Speechless" soloist. On the first chorus, the spot also illumines the trio. As the second verse begins, lights come up medium on choir and build as the song builds. As the song softens and becomes worshipful, the lights soften. The song ends soft and worshipful and lights fade as a spot comes up on the Narrator/Worship Leader.

"Eyes of Your Heart"/"Open the Eyes of My Heart"—Narrator/Worship Leader is spotlighted as he speaks. Lights come up on choir for "Eyes of Your Heart." As "Open the Eyes of My Heart" begins, lyric is projected for congregation to sing along. Be sure to do something to invite the congregation's participation. You could either verbally invite them or just motion to them to join in. Either the Narrator or the minister of music can serve as a worship leader for this song. You may even choose to have your worship team on the microphone with the choir during this song. Congregation also sings along on "Be Thou My Vision" as lyrics are projected.

"My Abba's Child"/"Abba Father"—As previous song ends, lights fade to dark and a spot comes up on the Narrator as he begins to speak. Children's choir processes in. (Directors can have little flashlights to help.) As Narrator finishes speaking, spot fades on him as lights come up on the Children's Choir. After "My Abba's Child" is completed, lights fade on children and spot comes up on Narrator. He tells the true story of Derek Redmond. Should you wish to add a visual accompaniment to this story, you could take slides of a track meet, runner's shoes running, a father embracing his son—whatever part of this story you would like to dramatize by using slides. As the story ends, lights dim and a spot picks up the soloist for the verse of "Abba Father." Then lights come up the children's choir.

This song climaxes as the lyrics of "Abba Father" chorus are projected. The soloist could serve as praise leader on this song, inviting the congregation to join in, or the minister of music may simply turn to direct the congregation. As the song ends, congregation is seated and lights gradually go down. Children exit.

"What Is Jesus Doing?"—A spot comes up on the Narrator as he begins speaking. (Children will still be in the process of exiting.) "What Is Jesus Doing" is a song that may be sung by a trio of youth or could be done by adults, if needed. Either two girls and a guy or three girls could be used. Spotlight comes up on solo, then duet, and finally trio. During second verse lights come up dim on choir. During this song you may choose to have a slide show spotlighting different ministries within your church, depicting the ways and places Jesus is at work in your body. It is especially effective to show familiar faces of people within the congregation doing the work God has called them to. As the song progresses into the congregational chorus, "Sometimes By Step," the lyrics are projected, and once again the Narrator or minister of music may serve as praise leader, or the trio may lead the congregation. During this congregational worship segment, the youth group could enter from every entrance with WIJD? (What Is Jesus Doing?) bracelets to hand out to the congregation while everyone is singing together, "Oh God, You are my God and I will ever praise You!"

"On My Knees"—As the previous song ends, the youth exit, lights fade, and a spot comes up on the Narrator. (During this sequence, especially, the Narrator's timing is a key to the effectiveness of the moment. He should mimic the recording as closely as possible. You wouldn't want to hear a train sound effect when the narrator is talking about prayer.) If using slides to visually portray the different ways we hear from God, a single slide each for "God's Word," "The Body of Christ Ministering to One Another," and "Prayer" could be effective. As the narration is finished, spot goes down on Narrator and up on soloist. All is dark except the spot on the soloist here. As choir comes in, dim lights come up on them. At the very end of the song when choir has finished singing, lights go back to dark with a spot on the soloist.

"When I Survey the Wondrous Cross"— Spot fades on previous soloist and comes up on Narrator as he tells the story of Henry Blackaby's family facing difficult circumstances. Lights then come up on the choir for the first two stanzas of "When I Survey." During the third stanza, lights fade on the choir. *Note: Choir must know this song by memory as this part of it will be done without lights.*

We suggest that your drama team could add depth to this musical moment in one of two ways:

1. Lights come up slowly on a crucifixion drama scene. Jesus is nailed to the cross, timing the striking of the hammer to the hammer hits recorded on the track. As choir sings "Did e'er such love...", the soldiers raise the cross into place and put the crown of thorns on Jesus' head. *Note: If pantomiming the crucifixion in this way, exact timing is important. The soldier nailing Jesus to the cross needs to line up his motion with the track so that each hammer blow occurs on beat one of measures 72 through 84. Measure 84 is the moment when the soldiers lift the cross, then place a crown of thorns on Jesus' head.*

2. Those with the ability to stage more difficult scenes may choose this second option. Rather than having only the crucifixion scene, two levels on the stage could be depicted: at the lower level, a family is circled around a hospital bed. Behind them at the upper level there is a crucifixion scene with Jesus already on the cross. As the last stanza of the song begins, lights come up on this scene, showing both levels. This would dramatize a family "looking at their difficult circumstances before the backdrop of the cross."

Invitation—Lights fade to dark. We strongly encourage you to utilize the video of Henry Blackaby to begin your invitation. If you and your choir view the video, you will see why. God has put an anointing on this man for this, his life message, and when he speaks, his words pierce the hearts of listeners to respond to God. As the video clip finishes, your pastor may want to come and preside over the invitation. Encourage your choir and orchestra members to have soft hearts before the Lord and feel free to respond themselves—they may be the catalysts for the entire congregation. Be ready to have your pianist and organist play hymns and choruses of invitation so that should you decide to extend the invitation beyond the music in the musical you will be well prepared for what the Lord wants to do. We recommend that you continue using whatever hymns and choruses you choose for a time before progressing into "Use Me, Send Me." The key is being flexible and not cutting off what God would want to do during this time. Lighting suggestions for the invitation time are as follows:

Invitation: As lights gradually fade to black after "When I Survey," begin to roll video. (If not using video, spot pastor or worship leader giving the invitation.) As the video ends (or the pastor begins to lead into the invitation), bring congregation lights up to medium, providing adequate light for the people to respond to the invitation.

"Use Me, Send Me"/"Have Thine Own Way"—These are two medleys of congregational songs that should be sung as part of the invitation. "Potter's Hand," which comes in the second half of the "Have Thine Own Way" medley, should be timed to wrap up the invitation time. Lyrics to all of these songs are projected.

Finale—As the invitation time ends, spot comes up on the Narrator/Worship Leader who leads into a closing prayer. At this point, either the Narrator or the minister of music will serve as worship leader for the song "I Will Never Be the Same" which will have lyrics projected. As the Finale progresses into the reprise of "Name of Names," banners process in with the names of God on them. A spot comes up on the trio. They lead out on "Speechless." During "Speechless," different soloists from the whole musical make their way to the front to join on microphone with the choir. Entire group reprise the last stanza of "When I Survey." As the last song cuts off, if appropriate, have the choir lead out in a clap offering to the Lord. This is a biblical way of showing our appreciation to God for all that He has done for us.

NOTES

NOTES

NOTES

NOTES

Experiencing God resources for group and individual study

Experiencing God: Member Book
This interactive workbook involves adults in daily study and weekly small-group sessions.
0-8054-9954-7 .... $12.95

Experiencing God: Leader Guide
For use in guiding small-group study.
0-8054-9951-2 ....$6.95

Experiencing God: Audiocassettes
Six tapes in album that feature messages by Henry Blackaby.
0-7673-1927-3 .... $29.95

Seven Realities of Experiencing God Video Series
For new and current Experiencing God participants. Two videos, 40 minutes each, support and enhance the group study.
0-8054-9853-2 .... $49.95

Experiencing God: Youth Edition
by Henry Blackaby and Claude King
Leads youth in a 10-week study of the Bible to learn how to know God better and how to know when God is speaking.
0-8054-9925-3 .... $9.95

Experiencing God: Youth Edition Leader Guide
Activities and teaching suggestions geared for youth.
0-8054-9924-5 .... $6.95

Experiencing God: Youth Edition Video Series
Two 90-minute videocassettes enhance group study and provide leadership training.
0-8054-9839-7 .... $49.95

Experiencing God for Preteens, Pupil Book
Nine sessions in workbook format for fifth and sixth graders.
0-8054-9859-1 .... $4.9

Experiencing God for Preteens, Leader Guide
Includes teaching plans to help older children focus on what Go plan is for their future.
0-8054-9860-5 .... $8.9

Spanish Adult Edition, Member Book
(Mi Experiencia con Dios)
0-7673-2369-6 .... $10.9

Spanish Adult Edition, Leader Guide
0-7673-2370-X........................... $6.9

Spanish Youth Edition, Member Book
0-8054-9845-1 .... $8.9

Spanish Youth Edition, Leader Guide
0-8054-9846-X........................... $6.9

Spanish Preteen Edition, Mem Book
0-8054-9850-8......................... $4.

Spanish Preteen Edition, Leade Guide
0-8054-9851-6......................... $8.

Korean Adult Edition, Member Book
0-7673-9328-7........................ $10.

To order, call 1-800-458-2772.

Or write: LifeWay Church Resources Customer Service,
MSN 113; 127 Ninth Avenue, North; Nashville, TN 37234-0113;
Fax: (615) 251-5933. Available at LifeWay Christian Stores.
Visit our website at www.lifeway.com.

Thank you for your order.

Prices and availability subject to change without notice.